Greek   grec

griechisch

griego   grčki

Have you ever had Greek food?

---

box   boîte

Box

caja   kutija

The box is full of clothes.

---

fire   feu

Feuer

fuego   vatra

Fire is hot.

rose   rose

Rose

rosa   ruža

Thank you for the rose.

nose   nez

Nase

nariz   nos

My nose is running.

night   nuit

Nacht

noche   noć

We sleep at night.

tree   arbre

Baum

árbol   drvo

She is sitting under a tree.

wood   bois

Holz

madera   drvo

He plays with wooden blocks

sister   sœur

Schwester

hermana   sestra

She is my sister.

song

chanson

Lied

canciones

pjesma

She is singing a song.

---

top

haut

oben

tapas

vrh

We like to play with tops.

---

bear

ours

Bär

oso

snositi

The bear likes to eat honey.

place   endroit

Ort

sitio   mjesto

This is my favorite place.

---

office   bureau

Büro

oficina   ured

Do you need any office supplies?

---

day   journée

Tag

día   dan

This day is the 30th.

Stock

stick · bâton · palo · štap

He is playing sticks.

Zuhause

home · maison · casa · Dom

He drew a picture of his home.

Auge

eye · œil · ojo · oko

He is closing his eyes.

chart　　　　　　　　　　graphique

Diagramm

gráfico　　　　　　　　　　grafikon

What does your medical chart say?

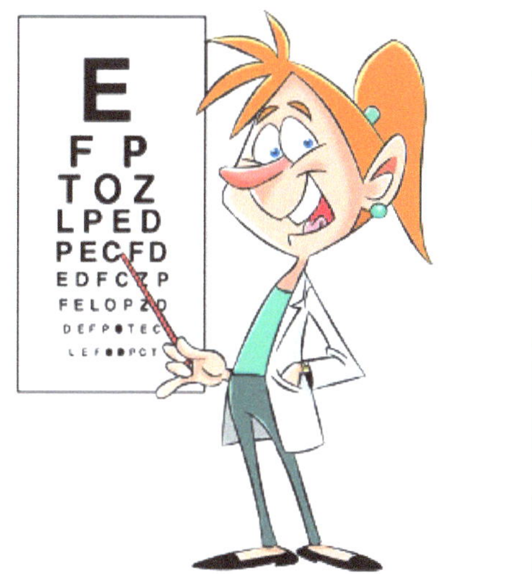

conditions　　　　　　　　conditions

Bedingungen

condiciones　　　　　　　　Uvjeti

What are the weather conditions.

cake　　　　　　　　　　gâteau

Kuchen

pastel　　　　　　　　　　torta

The cake is white and pink.

snow

Schnee

neige

nieve

snijeg

I have fun in the snow.

cotton

Baumwolle

coton

algodón

pamuk

A q-tip is made of cotton.

cat

Katze

chat

gato

mačka

That cat is adorable.

thing　　　　　　　chose

Ding

cosa　　　　　　　stvar

I am thinking of many things.

---

farmer　　　　　　fermier

Farmer

agricultor　　　　seljak

The farmer had a farm.

---

egg　　　　　　　oeuf

Ei

huevo　　　　　　jaje

The bunny has many eggs.

Wind

wind

vent

Wind

viento

vjetar

The wind blows the leaves.

Schuh

shoe

chaussure

Schuh

zapato

cipela

I have new shoes.

Name

name

nom

Name

nombre

Ime

My name is Joe.

children — les enfants

Kinder

niños — djeca

Four children sang.

---

score — but

Ergebnis

puntuación — postići

What was the final score?

---

children — les enfants

Kinder

niños — djeca

The children are playing.

boat   bateau

Boot

barco   čamac

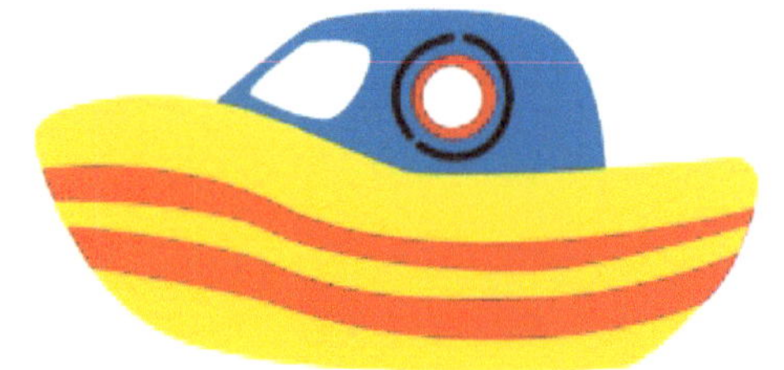

The boat is sailing.

---

nest   nid

Nest

nido   gnijezdo

The bird has a nest.

---

chair   chaises

Stühle

sillas   stolice

He is sitting on the chair.

corn — blé

Mais

maíz — kukuruz

I grow corn in the garden.

car — voiture

Auto

coche — automobil

My car is fast

brother — frère

Bruder

hermano — brat

They are brothers.

way   façon

Weg

camino   put

They find a way back home.

---

page   page

Seite

página   stranica

Please turn the page.

---

rope   corde

Seil

cuerda   uže

Do you have any rope?

picture · image

Bild

imagen · slika

He is taking some pictures.

doll · poupée

Puppe

muñeca · lutka

She is hugging her doll.

bird · oiseau

Vogel

pájaro · ptica

The bird is dancing happily.

coat   manteau

Mantel

saco   kaput

She is wearing her coat.

---

game   jeu

Spiel

juegos   igra

What game is it?

---

girl   fille

Mädchen

niña   djevojka

The girl is pretty.

hill   colline

Hügel

colina   brdo

The house is on the hill.

---

face   visage

Gesicht

cara   lice

They were at the face painting booth.

---

idea   idée

Idee

idea   ideja

I have an idea!

house
maison

Haus

casa
kuća

We live in the same house.

head
tête

Kopf

cabeza
glava

She has a hat on her head.

chicken
poulet

Hähnchen

pollo
pilence

The chicken is laying eggs.

toy   jouet

Spielzeug

juguete   igračka

He has a whole box of toys.

birthday   anniversaire

Geburtstag

cumpleaños   rođendan

Today is my birthday.

garden   jardin

Garten

jardín   vrt

They are going to the garden.

party

fête

Party

fiesta

Zabava

I love to go to parties.

---

watch

l'horloge

Uhr

reloj

sat

My watch is ticking.

---

seat

siège

Sitz

asiento

sjedalo

The girls took a seat in the sand.

leg

jambe

Bein

pierna

noga

My leg is feeling better.

---

ring

bague

Ring

anillo

prsten

The bird is holding a ring.

---

letter

alphabet

Alphabet

alfabeto

abeceda

Learn English letters is fun.

water   l'eau

Wasser

agua   voda

He is drinking water.

mother   mère

Mutter

madre   majka

My mother loves me.

school   école

Schule

colegio   škola

They are going to school.

boy   garçon

Junge

chico   dječak

The boy is eating dinner.

---

time   temps

Zeit

hora   vrijeme

He is telling the time.

---

example   exemple

Beispiel

ejemplo   primjer

This is an example of a bird.

sheep   mouton

Schaf

oveja   ovca

The sheep have fluffy wool.

---

apple   pomme

Apfel

manzana   jabuka

Apples are a popular fruit.

---

dog   chien

Hund

perro   pas

The dog wants to eat sweets.

man

homme

Mann

hombre

čovjek

This man is my dad.

---

bed

lit

Bett

cama

krevet

We all share three beds.

---

food

aliments

Essen

comida

hrana

They made a lot of food.

fish   poisson

Fisch

pez   riba

There are two fish.

family   famille

Familie

familia   obitelj

How big is your family?

father   père

Vater

papá   otac

He is a nice father.

door — porte

Tür

puerta — vrata

He is knocking on the door.

---

flower — fleur

Blume

flor — cvijet

She is holding a flower.

---

grass — herbe

Gras

césped — trava

The goat is eating the grass.

city

Stadt

ciudad

ville

Grad

He worked in the city.

---

seed

la graine

Samen

semilla

sjeme

We will plant the seeds.

---

rabbit

lapin

Hase

conejo

zec

The rabbit wants to play.

rain / pluie

Regen

lluvia / kiša

We love the rain!

---

street / rue

Straße

calle / ulica

They walk across the street.

---

paper / papier

Papier

papel / papir

I like to color on paper.

feet

pieds

Füße

pies

noge

His feet are swollen.

cow

vache

Kuh

vaca

krava

The cow is standing up.

church

église

Kirche

iglesia

crkva

Did you go to church?

bread pain

Brot

un pan kruh

She is baking some bread.

hoe houe

Hacke

azada motika

Use a hoe in the garden.

milk lait

Milch

leche mlijeko

The baby is drinking milk.

four

quatre

vier

cuatro

četiri

There were four of them.

---

baby

bébé

Baby

bebé

dijete

The baby is crawling.

---

ground

sol

Boden

suelo

tlo

It plays a trick on the ground.

France — france

Frankreich

francia — Francuska

Have you ever been to France?

kitty — minou

Kitty

gatito — mače

I like my kitty.

squirrel — écureuil

Eichhörnchen

ardilla — vjeverica

The squirrel is on the tree.

ball   balle

Ball

pelota   lopta

He is bouncing the ball.

---

horse   cheval

Pferd

caballo   konj

The horse is galloping.

---

fresh   frais

frisch

fresco   svježe

All the fruit is fresh.

money

argent

Geld

dinero

novac

I save money in my piggy bank.

company

compagnie

Unternehmen

empresa

društvo

What company do you work for?

sun

soleil

Sonne

dom

Sunce

The sun is very bright.

floor — sol

Fußboden

suelo — kat

The girl sits on the floor.

hand — main

Hand

mano — ruka

You should wash your hands.

duck — canard

Ente

pato — patka

The duck is swimming.

Bauernhof

farm · ferme · granja · farma

The farm has lots of animals.

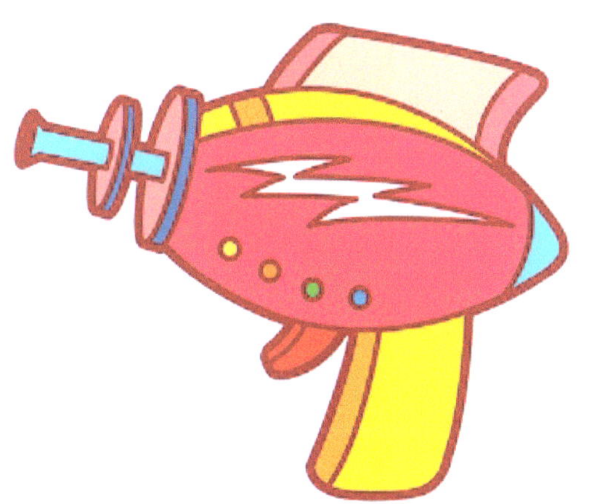

Gewehr

gun · pistolet · pistola · topovi

We played with a water gun.

Glocke

bell · cloche · campana · zvono

I hear the bell ringing!

Männer

men · hommes · hombres · muškarci

The men are arguing.

Sauerstoff

oxygen · oxygène · oxígeno · kisik

What is the symbol for oxygen?

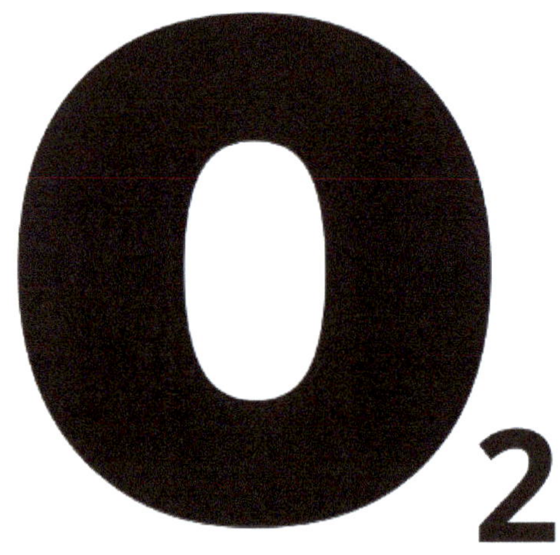

Schwein

pig · porc · cerdo · svinja

She is lying on the pig.

morning   matin

Morgen

mañana   jutro

I wake up in the morning.

---

column   colonne

Säule

columna   stupac

Did you read the newspaper column?

---

table   table

Tabelle

mesa   stol

There is a toy on the table.

robin   robin

Robin

robin   crvendać

The robin is helping Santa.

---

goodbye   au revoir

Auf

adiós   Doviđenja

The bear is saying goodbye.

---

window   fenêtre

Fenster

ventana   prozor

The window is open.